CLEAN-FREAK FULLY-EQUIPPED

VOLUME I

TOUYA TOBINA

D1004801

NO, NOT SHAME! YES! TOTALLY OCD!

Clean-Freak Fully-Equipped Volume 1

Created By Touya Tobina

Translation - Monica Seya Chin
English Adaptation - Lianne Sentar
Copy Edit - Jill Bentley
Retouch and Lettering - Star Print Brokers
Production Artist - Star Print Brokers
Graphic Designer - Seojon Lee

Editor - Lillian Diaz-Przybyl
Print Production Manager - Lucas Rivera
Managing Editor - Vy Nguyen
Senior Designer - Louis Csontos
Art Director - Al-Insan Lashley
Director of Sales and Manufacturing - Allyson De Simone
Senior Vice President - Mike Kiley
President and C.O.O. - John Parker
C.E.O. and Chief Creative Officer - Stu Levy

A TOKYOPOP® Manga

TOKYOPOP and are trademarks or registered trademarks of TOKYOPOP Inc.

TOKYOPOP Inc.
5900 Wilshire Blvd. Suite 2000
Los Angeles, CA 90036

E-mail: info@TOKYOPOP.com
Come visit us online at www.TOKYOPOP.com

KEPPEKI SHONEN KANZEN SOUBI by Touya Tobina © 2007 by Touya Tobina All rights reserved.
First published in Japan in 2007 by HAKUSENSHA, INC., Tokyo
English language translation rights in the United States of America and Canada arranged with HAKUSENSHA, INC., Tokyo through Tuttle-Mori Agency Inc., Tokyo
English text copyright © 2010 TOKYOPOP Inc.

All rights reserved. No portion of this book may be reproduced or transmitted in any form or by any means without written permission from the copyright holders. This manga is a work of fiction. Any resemblance to actual events or locales or persons, living or dead, is entirely coincidental.

ISBN: 978-1-4278-3017-3

First TOKYOPOP printing: March 2011

10 9 8 7 6 5 4 3 2 1

Printed in the USA

CLEAN-FREAK FULLY-EQUIPPED™

VOLUME 1

BY

TOUYA TOBINA

TOKYOPOP®

HAMBURG // LONDON // LOS ANGELES // TOKYO

CONTENTS

SANITIZED FOR YOUR PROTECTION

EPISODE 1 005
EPISODE 2 037
EPISODE 3 081
EPISODE 4 123

〈ONE-SHOT COMICS〉

DISPATCH STUDENT 159

〈BONUS〉

PARANOIA BOY, FULLY FAILING 174

ミャキー
BZZ BZZ
BZZ BZZ
It sure is hot today.
It's so hot it's bugging the crap out of me!
ARRIVING AT SCHOOL.
SATA SENDA (MALE).
GRADE 6.
SUMMER.
GERMA-PHOBE (SEVERE).
EPISODE 1

N
EPISODE
1

YOU'LL PICK UP GERMS IF YOU KEEP TOUCHING EVERYTHING, SWEETHEART.
I'm coooounting!
24!
I'm glad you're having fun, Sata.
23!
TAP
TAP
ARE WE ALMOST AT THE ROLLER-COASTER NOW?!
YEP! ALMOST.
IT ALL BEGAN DURING MY THIRD GRADE SUMMER VACATION.
A FUN FAMILY OUTING AT AN AMUSEMENT PARK TURNED INTO A NIGHT-MARE.
TREMBLE
NN...
BU...
WHA...
BU ...
ぐり
SQUISH

...I BEGAN TO FEAR EVERY PUBLIC ITEM I SAW IN TOWN.
H-HOW LONG WAS HE DOING THAT? DID HE TOUCH THIS POLE TOO?!
TWITCH
EVER SINCE THEN...
!!!
What're you doing?
TREMBLE
TREMBLE
SENDA!
IT WAS THE BEGIN-NING OF THE END.
IT WAS A FORMATIVE MOMENT OF HORROR IN MY LIFE.

OBSERVE MY PRESENT STATE.
YOU NEED TO DISCUSS THE CLASS TRIP WITH YOUR CLASSMATES!
GOAL.
MODERATION MAKES A HAPPY LIFE!
JUST GET IN YOUR GROUP!
IS THAT ALL? THEN LEAVE ME BE!
NO! I REFUSE TO GO ANYWHERE THAT HASN'T BEEN SANITIZED!
SHAKE
YOU'RE GOING ON THAT TRIP.
Your attendance sheet has mysteriously vanished.
THAT'S AN ABUSE OF YOUR AUTHORITY!
Class trip
will attend
will not attend
Year 6, class 2, Senda
I'VE ALREADY DECIDED NOT TO GO.
HE THINKS HE CAN FORCE ME TO GET BETTER.
BUT THE TRIP IS PART OF YOUR CURRICULUM, BOY!
School trip
Each group
Free time
YES! AND THAT WAS MY RIGHT!
SENDA, I KNOW YOU STAYED HOME DURING YOUR 5TH GRADE FIELD TRIP.
MY TEACHER
DOESN'T UNDERSTAND

I guess Senda is coming.
Crap.
He thinks we're all dirty.
They should let him stay home.
WHY DOES HE CARE? IT'S MY PROBLEM, ISN'T IT?
IT'S NOT FUN, BUT...
THE LONGER IT GOES ON...
...THE MORE MY PARANOIA MAKES ME FEAR EVERYTHING.
SCOOT
IRE IRE
HURRY UP AND MOVE YOUR DESK!
SKREEK
HE...HE DIRTIED ME.
.....!
HAT'S SICK! EOPLE ARE ONNA GET HE WRONG IDEA.
SIGH... I DON'T WANT TO GO.
YOU SHOULD BE GRATEFUL WE'RE EVEN LETTING YOU NEAR US, FREAK!
You make everything stink of alcohol!
UGH
HISS!
There's only so much sanitizer I can carry.
I CAN'T CHANGE THE WAY I SEE THE WORLD.
CALM DOWN, YAZAKI.
YOU TOO, SENDA.

We have to work together.
LET'S MAKE THIS THE BEST CLASS TRIP EVER!
...HOW CAN THEY POSSIBLY EXPECT ME TO HAVE FUN?
AND AS LONG AS I'M IN SURROUNDINGS THAT TERRIFY ME...
HA HA!
RIGHT, SENDA?
.....
UH... S-SURE, AIUCHI.
SHE'S SOOO CUTE.
WIPE
mumble
SPRITZ
WIPE
SPRITZ
HOW LONG ARE YOU GONNA KEEP SPRAYING THAT STUFF?!
UNTIL I'M DONE.
!!
AND THEN CAME THE FATEFUL DAY.
TOKYO STATI

GROUP 2 AND 4 ARE HERE, SIR!
THEN ALL THAT REMAINS...
SCRIBBLE SCRIBBLE
GROUP 5 IS ALL HERE.
GROUP 3 TOO.
MM.
GROUP 1'S ALL HERE.
OKAY.
GOOD.
NOW...
ONCE YOU ASSEMBLE YOUR GROUPS, LET ME KNOW.
OKAY!
Senda's holding us back, as usual.
...IS GROUP 6.
Sigh.
SPRITZ
HEY!
SPRITZ
IT'S SENDA!
...I think?
SHUU... KAAAH...
I DON'T THINK YOU'RE THIS CLASS, DARTH.
SHUU... KAAAH...
SHUU... KAAAH...
S-sorry to keep you waiting.
SHUU... KAAAH...

...I WON'T BE ABLE TO BREATHE.
N-NO!
DON'T!
TAKE THAT MASK OFF!
GET RID OF ALL THIS!
I've tolerated your behavior long enough!
YOU'D BETTER BE THE ONLY ONE WITH A HAZMAT SUIT!
What's wrong with you?!
YOU KNOW VERY WELL I'M THE ONLY ELEMENTARY STUDENT WITH SUCH ADVANCED EQUIPMENT.
Ha ha.
Pail
Pail
Pail
VERY FUNNY, SIR. IT'S ME--SENDA.
HUFF
SHUU KAAA
SHUU KAAAH
I KNOW.
I KNOW I'M OBSESSING ABOUT THIS.
BUT I CAN'T HELP IT.
IF MY TEACHER TAKES AWAY MY SAFETY EQUIPMENT...

ANNA...
YOU DON'T HAVE TO SIT NEXT TO HIM, Y'KNOW.
YEAH.
WHA?!
You're annoying, Yazaki!
YOU SHOULD SWITCH SEATS WITH OUR GROUP LEADER. COME ON, AIUCHI!
Come over here!
GROUP LEADER
YOU'RE FREAKING ME OUT.
I SURE HOPE YOU POKED HOLES IN THAT PLASTIC BAG. DO YOU HAVE A DEATH WISH?
I WISH THAT THING WASN'T SEE-THROUGH.
Your eyes are all glazed over.
WHAT'S WRONG, YAZAKI?
WELL...
You look worn out.
IT'S PROBABLY BECAUSE HE WAS SITTING NEXT TO SENDA THE WHOLE TRAIN RIDE.
I ORDER YOU TO TAKE THE HOT SEAT!
WHA?
That's what he gets for trying to make me do it.
Heh heh.
...WE MADE IT.

I KNOW THERE'S SOMETHING IN THIS ROOM!
huff
huff
SPRITZ
SPRITZ
SPRITZ
SPRITZ
TEACHER!
SPEAKING OF WHICH, IS SENDA ROOMING WITH US?
NOOO!
He's in our group, so yeah.
TAKE THAT BAG OFF YOUR HEAD BEFORE YOU SUFFOCATE.
SENDA ...
You're scaring everyone.
Or a serial killer!
He looks like a ghost!
!
BUT THERE ARE NINE PEOPLE SHARING THIS SPACE!
huff
DO YOU REALIZE HOW THAT COMPOUNDS THE RISK OF INFECTION?! I'M TRYING TO PREVENT TRANSMISSION HERE!
YOU'LL THANK ME WHEN YOU DON'T GET MRSA!
huff

I DON'T WANNA GO IN THERE!
Waaaah! Save us, teacher!
You already share a classroom with 35 people.
TAKE OFF THE BAG! HOW WOULD I EXPLAIN YOUR DEATH TO YOUR PARENTS?!
TWITCH
TWITCH
SPRI...
LET'S PLAY A GAME OF TELEPHONE AS A CLASS, ALL RIGHT?
Please separate into groups.
...WHAT, WE CAME ALL THIS WAY JUST TO PLAY A STUPID GAME?

DON'T THEY WORRY ABOUT ANYTHING?
THEY'RE ALL SO RELAXED... THEY'RE ENJOYING THEMSELVES.
Yay!
I DON'T GET IT.
IF NOT...
...THEN CAN I SIT NEXT TO YOU?
AREN'T YOU GONNA PLAY TELEPHONE, SENDA?
I'm kinda tired too.

SOMETHING ABOUT HAVING SOCIETIES.
THEY WERE TALKING ABOUT WHAT MAKES US HUMAN.
THAT MAKES SENSE, RIGHT?
I'm tired...
SHE'S STILL TALKING.
Maybe it's a girl thing.
OH, YEAH! I SAW THIS THING ON TV THE OTHER DAY.
...AND RECREATION IS A HARD WORD TO SAY, RIGHT?
blah
blah
SHE DIDN'T WAIT FOR MY ANSWER.
blah
JEEZ, PEOPLE ARE ALWAYS PAYING TOO MUCH ATTENTION TO ME!
blah
AND THAT TOURNAMENT, IT WAS SOOO LAME, SHE TOLD ME--
blah
すとっ
UMPH.

...MAYBE YOU'LL LOSE WHAT MAKES YOU HUMAN.
BUT THINK ABOUT IT.
IF "SOCIETY" MAKES US HUMAN, AND YOU KEEP PULLING AWAY FROM SOCIAL INTERACTIONS AND STUFF...

No! Don't make me flashback!
WHAT HAPPENED?

...YOU WEREN'T ALWAYS SUCH A NEAT FREAK.
I HEARD ...
.....

WELL ...
Hmm.
I DO KNOW...
...THAT EVERYONE'S GOT SOMETHING THAT SCARES THEM.
EVERYONE.
SO I THINK I CAN KINDA UNDERSTAND WHAT YOU'RE GOING THROUGH.
A-UCH!
Oh, right.
COMING!
What are you doing?
SO SHE DROPS A CRYPTIC MESSAGE AND SCURRIES OFF, DOES SHE?

I DIDN'T KNOW AIUCHI WAS POPULAR WITH THE OTHER BOYS.
Hee hee! Sebastian, let's race to the other side of the river!
Ha ha ha ha!
YOU...
...AREN'T HUMAN!
GASP
Senda Image.
I SUPPOSE SHE'S CUTE, IF I WANT TO BE OBJECTIVE ABOUT IT.
YAZAKI, YOU'RE UNRECOGNIZABLE WHEN YOU PUT YOUR HAIR DOWN.
GROUP LEADER, YOU'RE JUST A NERD.
If by "nerd" you mean "hot."
You're not human!
THE HEX
Thinking about it.
...SO THEN WHAT IS SHE AFRAID OF? I KNOW I SHOULDN'T CARE, BUT IT'S STILL KEEPING ME UP.
I'LL CALL IT THE AIUCHI CURSE.
Anti-bacterial bedding.
TRUE.
THE CUTEST GIRL IN OUR CLASS IS DEFINITELY AIUCHI.
?!
YEAH.
A lot of guys have crushes on her.
EITHER WAY, I HAVE TO FORGET ABOUT HER!
YOU SERIOUSLY THINK YOU'RE HUMAN?
HA!
THE HEX
Senda Image.
ARE THEY SERIOUS? MAYBE THEY'RE JUST TALKING IN THEIR SLEEP!
NO!
I THINK I'M GONNA TELL HER I LIKE HER ON THIS TRIP.
Maybe she'll go out with me!
KEEP DREAMING.
You'll make enemies!

OKAY.
ALL OF YOU GET INTO YOUR RESPECTIVE CLASS BUSES.
You're barely human.
SHE'S ONLY GOING TO BREAK MY HEART!
LET'S GO TO THE BACK OF THE BUS!
AIUCHI!
I WANTED TO SIT IN THE MIDDLE.
OH... SORRY, YAZAKI.
WHY? JUST COME JOIN ME!
I saved you a seat!
UH...
UM...
I THINK I FIGURED OUT YOUR FEAR, AIUCHI.

YOU'RE AFRAID OF THE BUS.
SHINE
DOLL
SENDA?!
WH-WHY ARE YOU DRESSED LIKE THAT? YOU LOOK LIKE A STALKER!
This is my Lighter transition gear.
See?
I instinctively braced myself!
MY OLDER SISTER GOES TO THE MIDDLE OF THE BUS TOO. APPARENTLY THE RIDE IS SMOOTHEST THERE.
Not sure if it's true.
!
SO YOUR OLDER SISTER GETS SICK ON THE BUS TOO?!
THAT'S A RELIEF!
THEY SELL MOTION SICKNESS MEDICINE, RIGHT?
SO IT CAN'T JUST BE YOU.
EALLY?! DIDN'T KNOW THAT!
I'M CARRYING SOME. WANT ONE?
EASE!
I THOUGHT IT WAS JUST ME.
RUSTLE
RUSTLE

SHAKA
I HATE HOW MUCH I RATTLE WITH ALL THIS STUFF.
WHOA-- YOU HAVE A TON OF PILLS!
HUH?
OH.
IT'S MOSTLY VITAMINS.
HERE.
TAKE IT!
THANKS, SENDA.
NOT AGAIN! I'M GETTING HEART PALPITATIONS AND SHORTNESS OF BREATH! CRAP! AND I DIDN'T BRING ANY CARDIAC MEDICATION!
BA-DUMP BA-DUMP BA-DUMP
HUFF
HUFF
HEY...
SENDA?

WE NEED TO GET YOU BACK WITH OTHER PEOPLE AGAIN.
Step one!
AS THANKS...
...I'M GONNA HELP YOU GET OVER YOUR FEAR OF GERMS.
.....
IN A WORLD WHERE EVERYTHING SCARES ME...
SENDA!
AIUCHI...
...WITH AIUCHI BY MY SIDE...

AND I WASN'T AFRAID ANYMORE.
...EVERYTHING STARTED TO SEEM BRIGHTER.
HOW CAN SHE DO THAT?
THIS IS TOTALLY FUN!
I've never seen anyone make such a mess while she eats.
SHUSH.
AND HOW DID I NEVER NOTICE IT BEFORE?
OH.
HEY.

SLAP
SENDA, YOU HAVE RED BEAN PASTE ON YOU TOO.
SO...
SORRY.

IF HE'S AFRAID OF DIRT, OF COURSE HE WOULDN'T WANT TO TOUCH MY HAND AFTER IT'S BEEN EVERYWHERE.
I WASN'T THINKING.
IT'S JUST...
I...
TEACHER!
My heart palpitations were by steps.
I-I THINK I'M DYING.
SIR...
NOW.
!
IT'S ANNA!
BA-DUMP BA-DUMP
BA-DUMP
YOU'RE SUFFOCATING. LOSE THE BAG.
Ungh...
GROSS! DON'T BARF HERE!
You're gonna make me barf too!
HOLD IT IN, AIUCHI!
!
SHE SAYS SHE FEELS SICK!
BART
IT'S OKAY, I'M CO--
DOES SHE NEED A VOMIT BAG?

Blrrgh!

SHIZUKA
BUT I CAN'T BELIEVE SENDA CAUGHT VOMIT.
Teacher's shirt.
WHOA.
THAT WAS A SUR-PRISE.
IT WAS A NICE CATCH.
ARE YOU FEELING BETTER NOW?
...
SNIFFLE
...
NGH.
...I'M S-SO SORRY!
...
SNIFF
I'M SORRY.
SENDA ...

MAN.
THIS SCHOOL TRIP WAS A DISASTER!
Group leader, this sucks! All my souvenirs won't fit!
Just push hard er.
ROOTN
WE STILL HAVE HALF A DAY LEFT.
DIDN'T YOU SAY YOU WERE GOING TO CONFESS TO AIUCHI TONIGHT?
HUH?!
NOT ANY-ORE!
SHE BLEW CHUNKS RIGHT IN FRONT OF ME!
Not exactly lady-like, right?
WHAT-EVER.
IT WAS DISGUST-ING AND IT BROKE MY HEART!
I'm so mad.
WHAT, A BODILY FUNCTION DISILLU-SIONED YOU?
I GUESS YOU COULD SAY THAT. I CAN'T BELIEVE SENDA RAN AND--
TIME TO DISILLUSION YOU AGAIN.

You're not going believe it!
CLACK
ANNA! LISA!
YOU HAVE TO COME SEE THIS!
STOP WORRYING ABOUT IT.
It was no big deal.
POUT
COME ON, ANNA.
I-I'M NOT READY TO GO OUT YET!
LEAVE ME ALONE!
C'MON.
YOU HEARD HER!
...WHAT'S WRONG WITH YOU, SENDA?!
POW
DRAG
NOOOOOOO!
YOU JUST CLAMMED UP AND DIDN'T SAY ANYTHING WHEN SHE BARFED, TOO!

ADMIT IT!
SHE TOTALLY GROSSED YOU OUT!
I DIDN'T SAY ANY-THING...
...BECAUSE I WAS SHOCKED THAT IT DIDN'T GROSS ME OUT!

TH-THANK YOU.

WHY MY HEART WON'T STOP POUNDING.
SENDA...
I GET IT NOW.
...I REALLY LIKE YOU.
I...
I...
...I LIKE YOU TOO!

HEY.
YOU KNOW WHAT TO-NIGHT IS?
NO ...
Always! Take them away from people!
And Nagatsuki don't bring your around!
IT'S THE NIGHT WE GET TO PLAY WITH FIREWORKS.
Romantic fireworks.
Stop following me!
AH. I SEE.
...Romantic?
WHY IS THERE SO MUCH SCREAMING OVER HERE?
Settle down, kids!
WHAT ON EARTH ARE YOU TWO MINORS DOING?!
GAAAAAH!
CRACK
Ew, this eye totally broke his glasses!
Illicit touching?! On a field trip?!
SO YOU ENDED UP GETTING IN A FIST FIGHT...
OH, WELL.
...AND I COULDN'T FIX MY PROB-LEM WITH MEDICINE.
OH.
About that...
YOU TOOK THE WRONG PILL.
IT'S MY FAULT. FOR... RESORTING TO VIOLENCE.
I'm sorry.
AND WE'RE STUCK IN HERE.
In time-out.

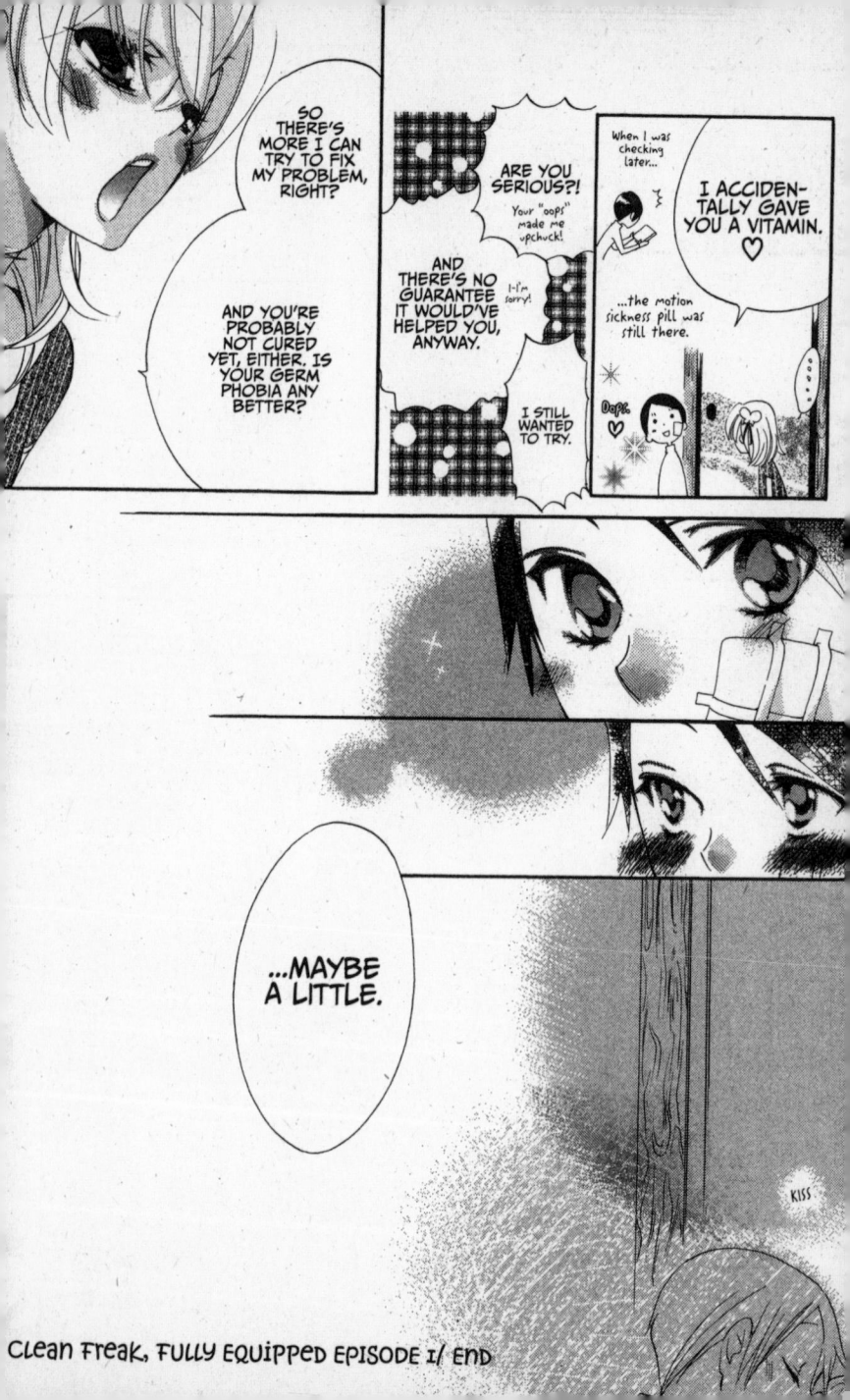

Clean Freak, Fully Equipped Episode 1/ End

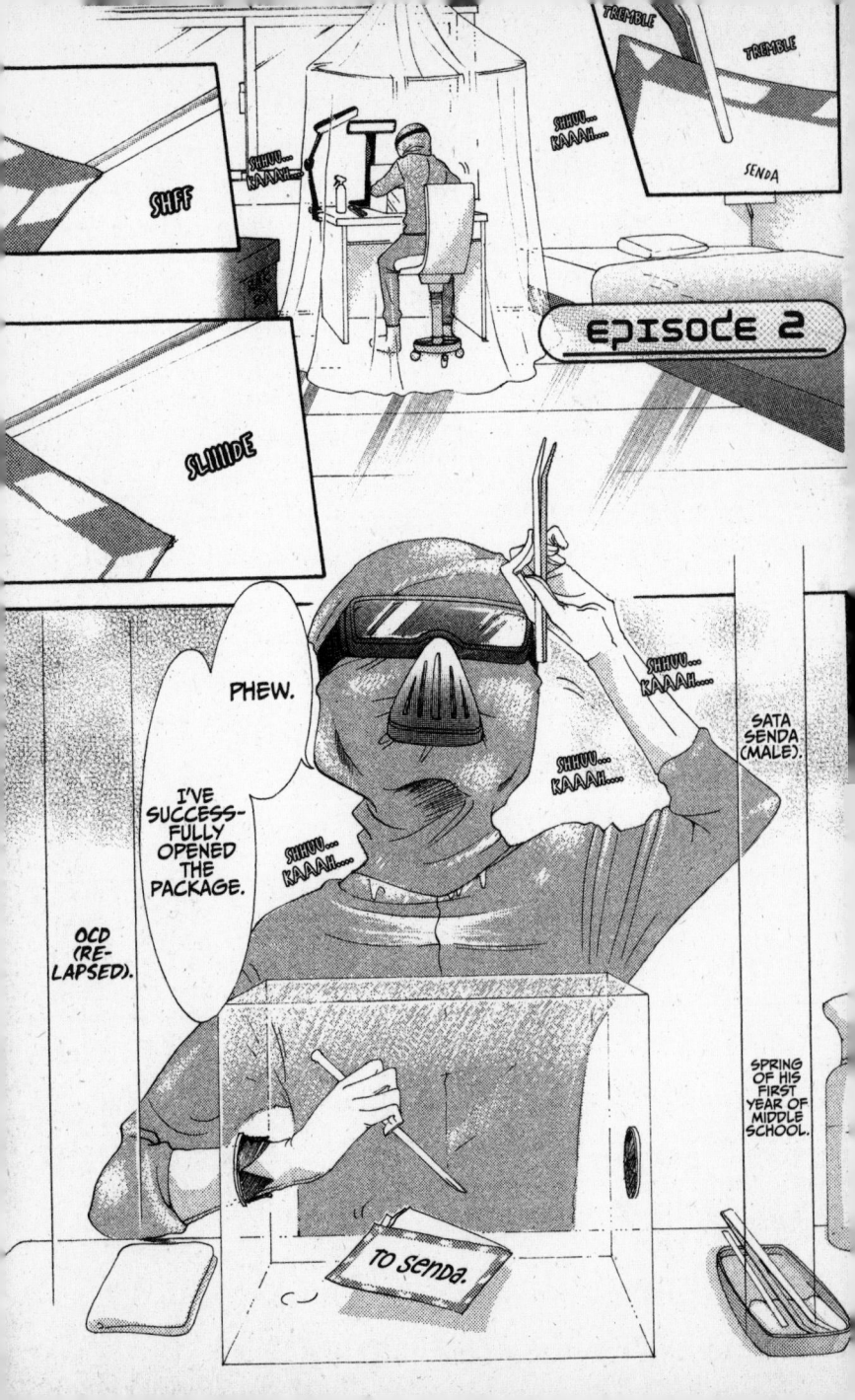
TRIEMBLE
TRIEMBLE
SENDA
SHIUU... KAAAA...
SHIUU... KAAAA...
SHFF
EPISODE 2
SLIIIDE
PHEW.
I'VE SUCCESS-FULLY OPENED THE PACKAGE.
SHIUU... KAAAA...
SHIUU... KAAAA...
SHIUU... KAAAA...
SATA SENDA (MALE).
OCD (RE-LAPSED).
SPRING OF HIS FIRST YEAR OF MIDDLE SCHOOL.
TO SENDA.

EPISODE
2

HEY! LOOK, SENDA!
WE CAN GET ON NEXT!
I'M SO PUMPED!
G-GOOD FOR US.
DO YOU REMEMBER THE LAST TIME WE WENT OUT TOGETHER IN THE SUMMER?
...TO THE HORRIFYING PLACE WHERE IT ALL BEGAN.
YOU INSISTED ON GOING...
CLANG CLUNK SKREE
Eek, I get the most excited right before getting on!

SQUASH
Woo!
Let's go!
They're going to sit here.
Not paying attention
Graduation.
I promise I'll write to you!
I HAVE TO MOVE BECAUSE OF PAPA'S JOB...
I'M GONNA BE IN NEW YORK FOR A WHILE.
AND IF THAT BIT OF COSMIC COINCIDENCE WEREN'T BAD ENOUGH...
IT...IT'S THE SAME GUY! AND HE BROUGHT A CLONE! WHY DOES THE UNIVERSE HATE ME?!
PLOMP
!!!
LET'S GET ON, SENDA!
He got on.
Dear Senda,
Things are good over here!
By the time this letter reaches you, you should be...
want to see your uniform...
Middle School
obably...
Meow.

I CAN'T EVEN TOUCH YOUR SWEET LETTERS DIRECTLY.
Unseen tears.
gleam
NOW ...
ALL NON-STERILE SURFACES ARE FREAKING ME OUT AGAIN. I'M AS BAD AS EVER.
Dear Senda, How are you? I'm doing really well!
As for me...I'm the same as always.
P.S. I'm sending you a picture of my friends and me in NY. From Anna.
NENE! GET THE CAMERA!
Dear Aiuchi, I'm glad you're well, but your picture is very confusing. Are you sure you're in New York?
ガチャ
カタン...
カリ
カリ
カリ
P.S.

BWA HA HA HA HA HA!
I'm looking forward to him being humiliated by this once he's grown up!
WE'RE TAKING A VIDEO NEXT!
You're a hoot, kiddo!
LOOK AT HIM, KAZUSA!
HA HA HA HA HA HA!
HE'S SO RIDICU-LOUS!
M-my sides hurt!
AH! Sata!
PFFFFTTT!
SATA!
DON'T FORGET YOUR SPRAY BOTTLES!
?!
SHIVER
Today is my first day of school... ...and it's raining water-borne pathogens.
OKAY.
SAY "CHEESE!"
It was supposed to be an entrance ceremony with cherry blossoms fluttering through the air.

ROLL
Sends Bolt
CLAP
CLAP
CLAP
CLAP
CLAP CLAP CLAP
THE NEW STUDENTS MAY NOW ENTER.
THAT GLARE IS COMEDY GOLD!
KEEP IT UP, SATA!
HUH?
CACKLE
I SWEAR I JUST FELT SOMETHING.
LIKE I'M BEING WATCHED.
ROLL ROLL ROLL ROLL
Sends Bolt
HA HA HA HA HA HA!
Aaah, can't breathe!
PFFFFT!
.....

SO I GUESS HE'S NOT JUST DOING IT FOR THE ATTENTION ...?
Not that we're looking.
Everyone's unspoken thought.
RODDDARRR
Senda Unit
EXCUSE ME! I'M NOT DOING THIS TO AMUSE YOU!
Stop making a mockery of my disorder!
I'M NOT DRESSED TYPICALLY FOR A MIDDLE-SCHOOLER, HUH?
MY NAME...
...IS YUI ANZAI! BUT YOU CAN CALL ME YUI!
I'VE GOT A LITTLE KID'S BOOTS AND SLICKER!
RIGHT?
SO WE CAN BE WEIRD TOGETHER, SATA-CCHI!

ゼェゼェ
I JUST THINK WE'RE MEANT TO BE FRIENDS! WHY WASTE TIME?
WA HA HA HA! ♡
I DON'T WANT A NICKNAME--I DON'T EVEN KNOW YOU.
WHO ARE YO CALLIN SATA-CCHI?
ARGH!
STOP SPLASH-ING FILTH INTO MY FACE.
IS HE ACTUALLY MAD AT ME?
BUT I WORE THIS RAIN-COAT SO I COULD SPLASH!
BWAAAAAH!
TREMBLE
TREMBLE
And he's crying!
HUH?

カタン
I HOPE IT RAINS TOMORROW TOO!
Fine now.
DON'T JINX ME! AND ARE YOU BIPOLAR OR SOMETHING?
SATA-GON!
ビチャッ
ビチャ
ビチャ
An entrance ceremony with cherry blossoms and rain...
...and a classmate who makes no sense whatsoever.
GON?!
GOOD MORNINK! ♡
Ugh--he found me.
MEOWWWWW! MEOW MEOW MEOW! ♫
ビチャ
バチャ
KYA HA HA HA HA HA!
STOP CONVULSING AND JUST WALK PROPERLY.
ARRRGH!
ぐる

ニキ
ガサッ
ハナ
SKWERK
RUSTLE
RUSTLE
TRASH CAN
Keep our hallways clean!
?
ROLL
RRRRRRRRRR
TCHAK
MEOW MEOW!
RRRRRRRRRRRRRRRRRRRR
DID HE REALLY BRING A HAIR-DRYER?!
To school?
SPRITZ
SPRITZ
HE DOES TAKE CARE OF THAT THING.
I'LL GIVE HIM THAT.
POM
POM
1 - 5

Pushing back and forth.
You do it!
Are you kidding me?
I'm not doing it. You pair up with him!
Take one for the team!
THAT NEVER GOES VERY WELL WITH ME.
I DON'T WANT THIS ANY MORE THAN YOU DO.
rumph!
Senda
I'M WORRIED ABOUT YOUR FUTURE.
SENDA.
LEASE STAY OUT OF IT.
THAT'S WHAT I USUALLY DO, ANYWAY.
PAIRS?
CHATTER
I guess I'll just pair up with the new teacher.
Well ...
Hm.
CRINGE
WE NEED A CLASS-WIDE ICEBREAKER. YOU'RE GOING TO GROW POTATOES TOGETHER!
FIRST ...
MY NAME IS MR. NAKATA. I'LL BE YOUR HOMEROOM AND SCIENCE TEACHER.
SO!
EVERYONE PAIR UP WITH A POTATO BUDDY.
LET'S TEAM UP!
streeetch
SATA-KYUN!

Broke through the barrier.
OOOH!
WHAT'S INSIDE THE BOX? LET ME IN!
"KYUN"?
WHAT DOES THAT EVEN MEAN?
...THAT ANYBODY CAME TO ME.
I WANNA TRY IT TOO!
!!
Still making it through.
YOU CAN'T COME IN.
WHAT?
THIS IS THE FIRST TIME SINCE MY PHOBIA STARTED ...
IT'S RAINING TODAY, SO YOU'LL ALL PLANT YOUR SEEDS TOMORROW.
OKAY!

New teacher, Nakata, 27 years old. Conflicted between his ideal and the reality that digging sucks.

After school.
YES, SIR!
HURRY UP AND COPY MY NOTES.
I DON'T CARE.
AND THEN, THE MAN-PIG MONSTER WENT "ROOOAR!"
...IT'S NOT LIKE I HAVE FRIENDS WHO WANT TO HANG AROUND OUTSIDE MY BOX.
I JUST HAVE NOTHING TO DO OTHER THAN STUDY.
SATA-PPE?
I'M GLAD YOU'RE SO SMART, SATA-PPE!
My grades are saved!
I MEAN...
WHATEVER.
UH...
WHAT? STOP THAT.

LET'S HANG OUT! OUTSIDE!
WHAT?!
BUT IT'S RAINING!
Exactly! Let's go!
No! H-he's incredibly strong!
MWA HA HA HA!
SAT-CCHIN?!
SAT-CCHIN! HURRY!
MY LOVE-CHILD WITH SATA-DON.
DON?!
AND YOU DIDN'T EVEN SHOW UP DURING PLANTING!
GLARE
LUVUUUUURVE
OOOH!
IS THIS IT? DID I FIND IT?
WATER MEANS DISEASE! AND MUD!
...I HATE RAIN, YUI ANZAI!
IN CASE YOU DIDN'T NOTICE...

SEE?
OUR BABY LOVES THE RAIN TOO.
Senda Unit
HE'S SO WEIRD.
REALLY... BIZARRE.
BUT FLOODING CAN STILL KILL THEM. WHAT THEY NEED IS MOD-ERATION.
WELL, YES.
PLANTS OBVIOUSLY LIKE RAIN BECAUSE THEY NEED IT.

LIAR.
YOU DON'T HAVE TO TAKE MY WORD FOR IT.
WHATEVER.
むくっ
OH, WELL.
NO WORRIES!

びちゃー
OOPS.
SORRY.
WHAM
YIPE
M-MURDERRRI-LAGHRRR!
Anger that can't be expressed in human words.
Snippets of sanity.
Owl!
STOP HITTING ME!
NEVER!
Nooooo!
You hit me first! With FILTH!
WAAAAH!
FSSSSH
AND NOW I HAVE TO USE THE SCHOOL'S UNFILTERED TAP WATER!
WHAT IS WRONG WITH ME?
I'M AN IDIOT! A TRUSTING IDIOT!
Very impressed.
YOU WEREN'T KIDDING ABOUT BEING A CLEAN FREAK!
WHOA...

HMMMM.
(SPRITZ)
S-SO MAYBE I HAVE A PROBLEM!
MAYBE I NEED PROFES-SIONAL HELP, OKAY?!
OH...I GUESS HE ADMITS IT.
Ouch.
サラ
サラ
サラ
!
I GUESS SO.
HEY, SATA?
FWAP

GO ...
...GOOD MORNING.
HUH?
IS HE TRYING NOT TO SPLASH ME?
GOOD MORNING!
YOU DON'T... HAVE TO DO THAT. JUST DON'T JUMP.
SOUNDS GOOD!
AND DON'T FLAIL!
ANZAI'S ABSENT TODAY AGAIN.
HM.
ARE YOU REALLY OKAY IN THIS RAIN?
I'M FINE.
JUST HURRY UP AND WRITE OUT NOTES.
I feel like I'm in Idaho.
I think so.
Is it growing okay?

IT'S SUNNY TODAY.
I WONDER...
...IF WE'LL GET ANY RAIN.
MUMBLE
ARGH!
WHAT'S GOTTEN INTO ME?!
ARE YOU GOING TO SCHOOL OR NOT?
QUIT BLOCKING THE DOOR!
WHACK
SIS
ざわ...っ
WH... SENDA?!
IS THERE A PROBLEM?
ER...
NO! I'M JUST...SURPRISED.
THANK YOU?
Senda
CAN ANYONE BRING ANZAI HIS HOMEWORK TODAY?

CLACK
SATA!
!
DING-DONG
OH.
NO, THANK YOU.
YOU WANNA COME IN?!
WHOA! YO TOTALLY SURPRISE ME!
THEN I'LL COME OUT!
homework
.....
MEDW MEDW
CLANG
CLANG
DOES HE LIVE ALONE?
LAUNDRY?
I NEED TO GRAB THE LAUNDRY!
HOLD ON A SEC-OND

SORRY THAT TOOK SO LONG.
YOU DON'T LOOK SICK TO ME, YUI ANZAI.
JUST CALL ME YUI!
WELL, MY DAY JUST ISN'T THE SAME WITHOUT IT!
SO YOU'RE JUST SKIPPING SUNNY DAYS? WHY?
BECAUSE PEOPLE MAKE FUN OF ME IF I WEAR MY AWESOME RAINCOAT IN THE SUN!
YOU...WEAR THAT RAINCOAT EVERY DAY?
WAIT.
YUP! BUT MY CLASSMATES IN GRADE SCHOOL MADE FUN OF ME ON WARM DAYS, SO NOW I JUST SKIP.
YOUR PRIORITIES CONFUSE ME.
STORY TIME!
DURING THE RAINY SEASON OF 2ND GRADE...
"YUI, SWEETHEART."
"YOU'RE SOAKED!"
!

"WE WERE..."
"WE WERE HAVING SO MUCH FUN I..."
"I..."
"I-I'M SORRY!"
"I WAS P-PLAYING WITH TAKA..."
ポタ ポタ
ポタ ポロ ポロ ポロ
...NOT TO BOTHER HER TOO MUCH.
SNIFF
SOB
"WAH!"
"I'M SO SOOOORRY!"
MY MOM'S A CAMERA OPERATOR WHO FLIES AROUND THE WORLD
I ALWAYS TRIED...
"DON'T APOLOGIZE. I'M HAPPY, BABY."
"YOU'RE A KID. YOU CAN GET AS DIRTY AS YOU WANT."
"YOU DON'T HAVE TO TRY TO BE A PERFECT CHILD JUST FOR MY SAKE."
"YUI."
I LEARNED...
RUB RUB

"THERE. NOW YOU CAN GET DIRTY AND BE A LITTLE BOY."
"STILL..."
"I DON'T WANT YOU TO CATCH A COLD WHILE I'M GONE."
...THAT BEING QUIET AND STAYING OUT OF TROUBLE ...
...ISN'T WHY PARENTS LOVE THEIR KIDS.
"EVEN WHEN I'M NOT AROUND!"
"THIS IS FOR YOU!"
I HAVEN'T HEARD FROM HER SINCE.
LATER, A CIVIL WAR BROKE OUT IN THE PLACE MY MOM WAS WORKING.
AND THAT'S HOW MY MOM GAVE ME MY SLICKER AND BOOTS.
"WOO!"
"THANKS, MAMA!"
"I'LL WEAR IT!"
"WHEE!"
"OKAY!"

...IS SHE OKAY
I'M SURE SHE'S FINE!
BUT MY RAINCOAT'S TAKING HER PLACE FOR NOW.
JUST UNTIL SHE COMES BACK!
I... GUESS IT MAKES SENSE?
!
.....
HE WANTS TO WEAR THE JACKET HIS MOM GAVE HIM.
YUI ANZAI...
...IS TRYING TO DISTRACT HIMSELF FROM WORRYING ABOUT HER.

I'M PRETTY SURE THERE ISN'T A SCHOOL RULE AGAINST IT.
YOU KNOW... WEARING A RAINCOAT ON A DRY DAY.
NOT THAT I KNOW OF, AT LEAST.

HI, SATA!
NICE DAY, HUH?
SATA!
UGH, THAT BOY HAS NO MANNERS!
……
ISN'T THAT NICE, SATA?
IT'S SUPPOSED TO BE SUNNY TODAY.
SUNNY …
…I GUESS HE WON'T COME TO SCHOOL TODAY.
MORNING!

SENDA
SATA.
SAAA-ATA.
M-MORNING ...
...YUI.
DO IT RIGHT, SATA!
DIIIIING DOOODONG
!

ガラ ガラ.
OH.
THERE'S YUI.
WE HELPED YOU A LOT IN ELEMENTARY SCHOOL, RIGHT?
SO WHY?
WHY WOULD YOU RATHER HANG OUT WITH THAT FREAK NOW?!
THEY MUST BE HIS OLD FRIENDS.
Unit
THEY'RE PRETTY RUDE.
Maybe I should step in...
WELL, C'MON!
I-V

I FEEL SORRY FOR THE GUY!

Yui was initially supposed to have sunlight allergies. I loved the ideas of him getting freckles and moles from that. I also really like all the school uniforms I get to draw. One of these days I want to draw some impossible school uniform.

WELCOME HOME, SATA.
DID YOU GET CAUGHT BY THE RAIN?
HE ALWAYS PISSED ME OFF.
IT ALL PISSES ME OFF.
ALL OF IT.
SCRUB
SCRUB
ALL OF IT.

WHY AM I LETTING THIS BOTHER ME?

OR ANY OF THEM.
!
SCOOT OVER!
OR HIM.
IF SHE SAID IT.
I DON'T THINK I'D BE SO ANGRY.
MAYBE IT'S BECAUSE OF WHERE THAT PITY IS COMING FROM.
ISN'T THAT...
ANZAI!
BUT THEY DIDN'T SAY IT.
HE DID.
FOR HIM TO SAY HE WAS BEING SOCIABLE WITH ME OUT OF PITY...
AND FOR A BRIEF MOMENT, I ACTUALLY THOUGHT OF HIM AS A FRIEND.

!
WHAT THE HECK ARE YOU DOING?!
!
I THOUGHT YOU DIDN'T BELIEVE ME!
WHAT? OF COURSE I BELIEVED YOU!
YOU SAID TOO MUCH WATER WILL KILL IT, RIGHT?!
I DON'T WANT IT TO DIE!
I DON'T WANT MY BEST FRIEND'S BABY TO DIE!
AND I DON'T...

THAT'S...
!
THAT'S HIS RAIN-COAT.
SPLASH
!
I-V

?
WHAT'S IMPORTANT TO MY BEST FRIEND...
...IS IMPORTANT TO ME TOO.

SATA...
!...!
1-V
YOU'RE DRENCHED.

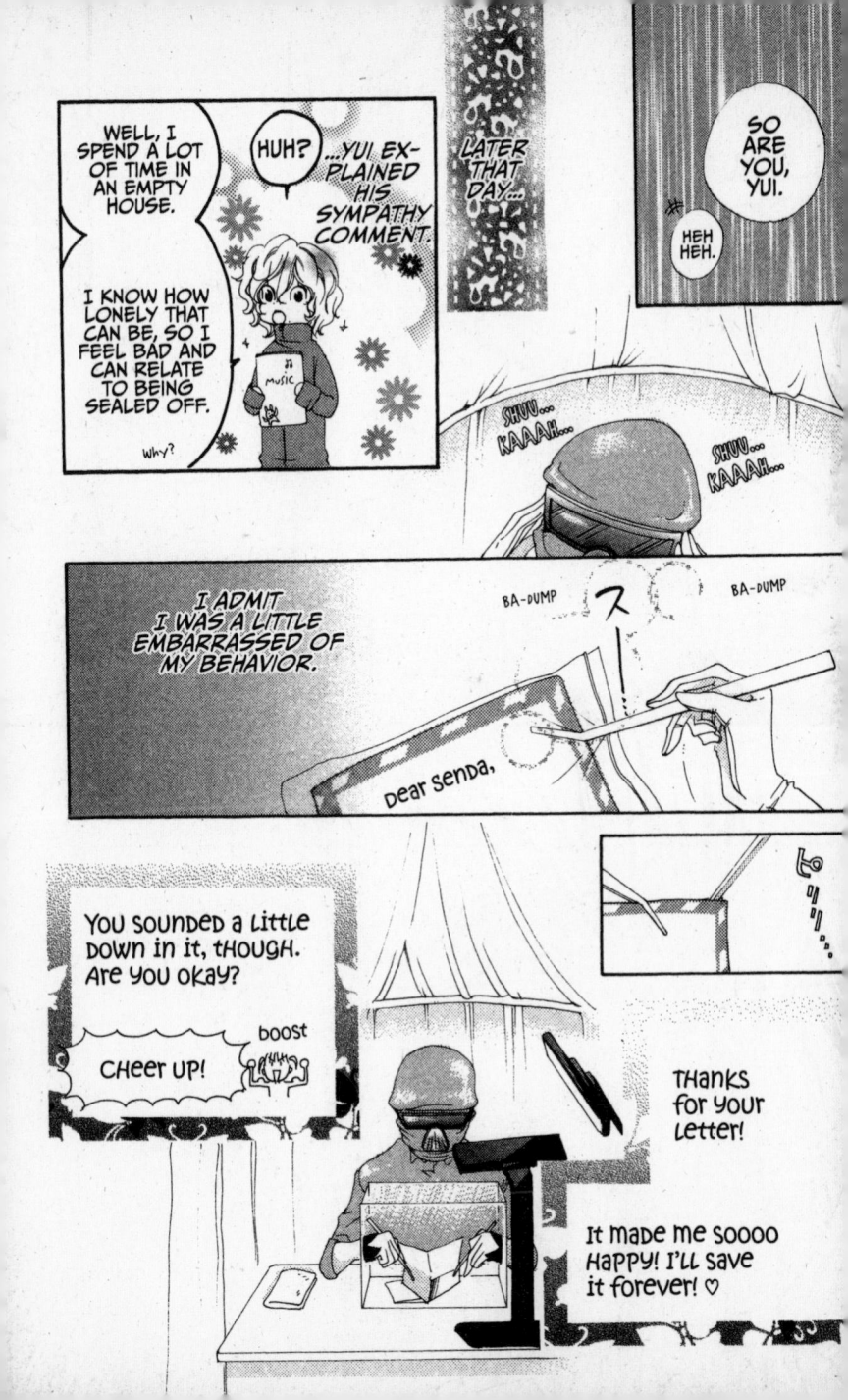
WELL, I SPEND A LOT OF TIME IN AN EMPTY HOUSE.
I KNOW HOW LONELY THAT CAN BE, SO I FEEL BAD AND CAN RELATE TO BEING SEALED OFF.
Why?
HUH?
...YUI EXPLAINED HIS SYMPATHY COMMENT.
♫ MUSIC
LATER THAT DAY...
SO ARE YOU, YUI.
HEH HEH.
SHUU... KAAAH...
SHUU... KAAAH...
I ADMIT I WAS A LITTLE EMBARRASSED OF MY BEHAVIOR.
BA-DUMP
BA-DUMP
Dear Senda,
YOU SOUNDED A LITTLE DOWN IN IT, THOUGH. ARE YOU OKAY?
CHEER UP!
boost
THANKS FOR YOUR LETTER!
IT MADE ME SOOOO HAPPY! I'LL SAVE IT FOREVER! ♡

Oh, and did you become friends with that "weird classmate" you were talking about? I hope so!
You two can bond over being weird.
P.S.
When I told my friends in NY about you, they said they really wanted to meet you!♡
Anna.
Aiuchi:
カサ カサ
そ…
カタン
Reading your letter reminds me of what a small world we live in. Thank you for that.
Please take care. Thank you again for the letter.
And don't worry about me. Your letter has given me new confidence.
Pumped up
I'm energized!
But let me add that I'm a little afraid that your (temporary?) new friends in NY are going to maim and/or devour you.
Seriously...
!
SATA!

GOOD MOON-ING!
YUI?
WHAT HAPPENED TO YOUR COAT?
Mwee Hee Hee.
Um... what?
てっ
てっ
てっ
I DON'T NEED IT ANYMORE 'CAUSE I HAVE YOU!
P.S.

CLEAN FREAK, FULLY EQUIPPED EPISODE 2 / END

EPISODE
3

A banana? Seriously?
You should've just said it was made of chocolate.
It's not a cigar--it's a poorly drawn banana! Banana!
No, no!

ROLL
ROLL
I'M BACK!
SEND.
SENDA!
DID YOU MISS ME?

SENDA!
AI...
Ü...
CHI?
LOOK WHO else I brought!
YAAA-AAAAH!
ECHO

RATTLE
RATTLE
RATTLE
RATTLE
RATTLE
AAAAAAAAAAAAAAAH.
BOY, THESE MORNINGS SURE HAVE GOTTEN WARM!
AAAAAH!
GAA
AAAA AAAA AAAA AAAA AAAAH.
HUFF
HUFF
HUFF
HUFF
I-I THOUGHT...
.....
SATA SENDA, 1ST YEAR MIDDLE SCHOOL STUDENT. IN THE DEAD HEAT OF SUMMER.
CLEAN FREAK (AND DANGEROUSLY DEHYDRATED.)
...I THOUGHT I WAS GOING TO DIE.

FOUR YEARS AGO...
His minions.
Booger king.
BUT THEN, A GRADE SCHOOL CLASSMATE NAMED ANNA AIUCHI CAME TO RESCUE ME FROM MY PARANOID, GERMAPHOBIC STATE.
You wanna go back to being human, right?
...DUE TO A CERTAIN NIGHTMARISH EXPERIENCE, I BECAME A NEAT FREAK. NOT EVEN A MOSQUITO COULD BREAK MY STERILITY SEAL.
See ya!
UN-FORTUNATELY, SHE SOON MOVED TO N.Y. (?), AND I RELAPSED BACK INTO MY DISORDER.
Waaaah!
Senda
TO THINK I WOULD DREAM OF AIUCHI SO CLEARLY.
IS IT BECAUSE I HAVEN'T HEARD FROM HER SINCE I SENT MY LETTER?
CLANG
ODD.

HMPH.
ROLL ROLL
Senda Unit
SHE'S PROBABLY BUSY WITH HER (NON-HUMAN) FRIENDS IN HER (NON-PERMANENT) RESIDENCY IN N.Y. AND HAS FORGOTTEN ALL ABOUT ME.
OH, WELL.
I'VE BEEN BUSY WITH MY OWN DIS-TRACTIONS.
HEY...!
LET'S...!
WOMEN CAN BE CRUEL...
...PLAY!
SATA!
BWA HA HA HA!
STOP IT!
WA HA HA HA!
ARGH! LET GO!
SPIN SPIN
Senda

THROUGH A BIZARRE SET OF CIRCUMSTANCES INVOLVING A PRIZED RAINCOAT...
...I NOW HAVE A BEST FRIEND NAMED YUI ANZAI.
NYA HA HA HA HA!
BAAAAARF!
Sick!
Ew! Senda threw up!
WHOA.
Infirmary
PLUG
WHEE!
WHEEZE
WHEEZE
UGGGGGH.
WHAT?! YOU CAN'T JUST BREAK UP WITH ME LIKE THAT!
Don't make me kill you!
Dooh.

GIMME SOME SORT OF EXPLANATION!
?!
YOU WANT A REASON? FINE.
IT'S JUST THAT TIME AGAIN.
TIME?
WHAT'S THAT SUPPOSED TO--
IT'S TIME FOR A CHANGE.
I NEED A NEW WARDROBE...
...AND I DEFINITELY NEED A NEW BOYFRIEND. ♡
ISN'T THAT OUR CLASSMATE YUMENO?
Girls are scary!
HUH?

SONOKO YUMENO?
THAT'S HER?
OH! DO YOU KNOW HER?
……
HRM... I GUESS PEOPLE CHANGE IN SIX YEARS.
specific example.
ARE YOU IGNORING ME? BOO!
OH, WOW.
YOU BROKE UP WITH THAT UPPERCLASSMAN?
1-5
YUP. ♡
DUNNO. I LOST COUNT.
HOW MANY BOYS DOES THAT MAKE?!
YOU'RE A TERRIBLE PERSON!
You don't remember?!
HUH? WHY?
Argh!
LIKE THIS IS NEWS.
KNOWING YOU, YOU ALREADY HAVE YOUR EYE ON YOUR NEXT TARGET. SO WHO'S THE LUCKY SUCKER THIS TIME?
!!!

I WANT SENDA. ♡
YES! TELL US!
YOU REALLY WANNA KNOW?
RAAAAAGH!
It had better not be my Inukai, either!
It better not be Mera!
TARGET.
WHA?!
LOCK-ON!

DURING THE ELEMENTARY SCHOOL TRIP, SENDA (LOUDLY) CONFESSED HIS LOVE TO AIUCHI IN FRONT OF EVERYONE.
THEN YOU KNOW ABOUT HIM SCREAMING HIS LOVE FOR ANOTHER GIRL.
THEN YOU KNEW HIM WHEN WE WERE IN ELEMENTARY SCHOOL, RIGHT?
PLEASE STOP TALKING OVER THERE!
Huh? He screamed his love?!
OF COURSE I KNOW.
Not to judge, but... we're gonna judge!
Did you not notice that he's hermetically sealed?!
ARE YOU SERIOUS, SONOKO?!
SETTLE DOWN, PLEASE.
He lives in a box!
HOW RUDE.
THAT'S NOT A THING!
SURE WE DO...WE WERE IN THE SAME CLASS IN PRE-SCHOOL.
YOU TWO HAVE NOTHING IN COMMON!
WAIT.
IF YOU JUST WANT HIM BECAUSE HE'S A CHALLENGE, TAKE MY ADVICE AND DROP IT.
Be quiet!
What's she like? Tell me about your girlfriend!
THAT'S IF IT'S ACTUALLY WORTH HAVING!
BUT NOTHING WORTH HAVING EVER COMES EASY.
.....
Heh.

Hey.
Wha?
It looks like Senda's get-up is for UV protection.
I've seen housewives all covered up outside, but...
squeak
I'm telling you, he's just really scared of the sun!
He's definitely doing it to block out germs.
DROP
Oops.
UV Protection
He did everything to keep from getting sunburned.
Then it wasn't the germs.
Hate.
Just kidding! His mortal enemy is still germs. Drawing him with sunglasses and the mask may confuse people, though.
I KNOW EVERYONE AVOIDS HIM NOW BECAUSE HE'S SUCH A GERMAPHOBE.
WHOA.
HARD TO BELIEVE.
Meow!
HMM...
BUT I WAS IN HIS CLASS IN PRESCHOOL TOO.
SENDA WAS PRETTY POPULAR BACK IN THE DAY.
SERIOUSLY?
I'M SORRY, BUT THERE'S NO LOGICAL REASON WE SHOULD DATE.

LOGICAL REASON?
YOU DON'T NEED A REASON TO FALL IN LOVE.
HM.
TAKE YOUR FEELINGS FOR AIUCHI, FOR EXAMPLE.
DO YOU HAVE A LOGICAL REASON FOR LIKING HER?
WHAT PARTS OF AIUCHI DO YOU LIKE?
!!
HEY!
WHO'S AIUCHI?
SHUT UP!
THAT'S NOT AN ANSWER.
UH ...
LET ME MAKE THIS EASIER FOR YOU.
...A-A-AIUCHI IS...UM... A SPECIAL CASE!

smile of an angel.
Tee hee hee!
YOU WON'T BE HUUUUMAN ANYMORE!
HER...PERSONALITY?
Voice of the devil.
.....
Senda's totally weird!
N.Y.!!
N.Y.
HER... COMMENTS?
.....
I...I HAVE NO IDEA WHY I LIKE HER!
WHAT IS LOVE, ANYWAY?
BUT...
Dear lord!
WAS I CHARMED BY SOMETHING SUPERFICIAL? DID I RELINQUISH MYSELF TO ROMANCE FOR ROMANCE'S SAKE?!
What does it mean to love someone?!
What parts of me do you like?
Sora! What about me?
SEE?
PARTS?
OF AIUCHI?

YOU DON'T KNOW WHY YOU LIKE HER.
MAYBE YOU WERE JUST ATTRACTED TO HER.
WHICH MEANS YOU CAN DEVELOP AN ATTRACTION TO ME.
!!!
Girls are scary.
I can't believe she said that!
She's so... aggressive.
ガッ
GLANCE
WHAT?
GLANCE
THIS IS DISTURBING.
WHAT ARE YOU DOING, SATA?
カサ
カサ
I'M TRYING TO COOK.

I CAN'T FIGURE OUT WHY I'M IN LOVE WITH AIUCHI.
ANTSY
A, UM, HAND-WRITTEN LETTER?
ANTSY
DID YOU NOTICE...
...IF I GOT A LETTER FROM SOME-ONE?
OH.
FROM AIUCHI?
N-NO! THAT WASN'T WHAT I WAS ASKING! AT ALL!
WE DIDN'T GET ANY-THING FROM AIUCHI TODAY.
.....
FOR-GET I SAID ANYTHING!
BON APPÉTIT!
Milk

I HATE CARROTS.
SHE'S PERSISTENT.
And in my personal space.
Pok
Mama special
FLICK
IF YOU DON'T APPRECIATE ALL FOOD, THE WASTE GHOSTS WILL COME FOR YOU.
DON'T BE SO PICKY, SENDA.
Carrot that was put aside.
You always seem to bring it.
DO YOU EVER BUY YOUR LUNCH, SENDA?
OF COURSE NOT.
THE ONLY FOOD I'M WILLING TO EAT IS FOOD THAT WAS PREPARED UNDER MY SUPERVISION.
Mama special
Mom's joke.

EXCUSE ME?
OH.
munch
!
YUMENO...
SO YOU LIKE BROCCOLI NOW?
Senda Unit
TREMBLE TREMBLE

YOU... REMEMBER THAT?

WELL...

IT'S TRUE THAT PEOPLE CAN CHANGE A LOT IN SIX YEARS.

PRIME EXAMPLE.

Hey, wait up!

See ya!

Ha ha ha! Try to catch me!

You wanna come over and see my cat?

I'm allergic, duh.

のっそり

RIGHT.

OUT... TIME.

OUT TIME!

SENDA!

LET'S WALK HOME TO-GETHER.
!
SHOVE
.....
WHY?

WHY ARE YOU DOING THIS TO ME?!
YOU KNOW I DON'T LIKE PEOPLE TOUCHING ME!
EVEN IF I WAS...
...I COULDN'T TELL YOU WHY!
WHAT?
YOU'D BE FINE WITH IT IF I WAS ANNA AIUCHI!
IS SHE... RIGHT?
WOULD I LET AIUCHI TOUCH ME LIKE THAT?
I...
.....!

YOU OKAY?
GO AWAY!
I HATE TINY GUYS. ESPECIALLY ONES WITH FRECKLES!
SORRY ...
BUT I REALLY LIKE SATA.
I THINK I SHOULD BE FRIENDS WITH ANYONE ELSE WHO LIKES HIM TOO.
HUH?
LEAVE ME ALONE!
I DON'T ACTUALLY LIKE THAT WEIRDO, OKAY?!
.....
BUT YOU LOOK SO LONELY.
SEE?

YOUR FACE GIVES YOU AWAY.
THE TRUTH IS...
.....
"OKAY, KIDS!"
"...THAT WE ALL MADE TOGETHER."
"IT'S TIME TO EAT THE STEW..."
THE TRUTH IS...
IT WAS DURING OUR OVERNIGHT CAMPOUT...
"YOU CAN'T EAT BROCCOLI, SONOKO?"
IT HAPPENED BACK IN PRE-SCHOOL.
!
びくっ
モグ
モグ
ぐり
ぐり
JUSTICE
Using a fork is hard.

CHOMP
"SATA!"
"I HATE BROCCOLI!"
"I HATE IT!"
"JEEZ."
"IT'S NOT MY FAULT IF THE TEACHER CATCHES YOU SHARING GERMS."
Covering up.
"HA HA! WE'LL ALL GET IN TROUBLE!"
.....
"SONO-KO."
"IF YOU DON'T EAT ALL YOUR FOOD..."
"...THE FARMERS ARE GOING TO TURN INTO WASTE GHOSTS AND COME FOR YOU."
!!
"RE-MEMBER THAT!"
"N-NO!"
Now I'm scared!
They're very scary.
Is that true?!
They're scary and strong.
"ACK!"
Something's different.

"I DON'T LIKE GHOSTS!"
"NOT TO WORRY!"
"IF YOU CAN FORCE YOURSELF TO EAT A TINY BIT..."
"...I'LL EAT THE REST FOR YOU."
It can be our secret.
"EXCELLENT WORK, SONOKO!"
"EXCEL-LENT."

SINCE THEN, SENDA HAD A SPECIAL PLACE IN MY HEART.
BUT...
...BACK THEN, HE ALWAYS HAD A LOT OF FRIENDS.
AND...
...HE CHOSE SOMEONE ELSE.
I WANTED HIM TO NOTICE ME.
SO I CHASED AFTER OTHER BOYS TO TRY AND GET HIS ATTENTION.
AND NOW...

HE CHOSE SOMEONE ELSE...!
ガチャ
WELCOME HOME, SATA.
SPRITZ
SPRITZ
SPRITZ
.....
SPRITZ
!
SPRITZ
SLAM RUSTLE
BANG
SPRITZ

I NEED TO PREPARE A CLEAN ROOM IMMEDIATELY!
IT COULD BE INFECTED!
AGH! H-HELLO, MOM! HELLO!
PLEASE DON'T--I MEAN...
I WONDER WHAT'S INSIDE?
I DON'T CARE, BUT--
JUST OPEN IT!
NO!
NO!
WAIT!
LITTLE BOYS WHO CAN'T TELL THEIR MOTHERS "HELLO" WHEN THEY COME IN...
You're such a rude child.
It's the only way you'll learn.
I'll have to destroy this.
...DON'T DESERVE PACKAGES FROM THEIR GIRLFRIEND OVERSEAS.
?!!
Some thing yummy?
I want to see what's inside.
Hurry!
Mom, drop the Package!
Senda shield unit 1
A DVD-R?
I GUESS VIDEO LETTERS ARE ON DVD NOW.
AW ...
Too bad.
Heh heh
PLEASE VACATE THE PREMISES
Now!

Close-up of the window.
CLICK
UH...
WHERE EXACTLY DID SHE FILM THIS?
I'M REALLY MAD AT YOU RIGHT NOW.
SHOULD I START WORRYING ABOUT HER? SHE'S ALWAYS SURROUNDED BY CARNIVORES!
PANIC
I'M GONNA BE HONEST.
TREMBLE
Distracted from the message.

HUH?

.....
AND!
AIUCHI ...
YOU JERK!
SHE WAS NERVOUS ABOUT OUR LACK OF COMMUNI-CATION TOO.
I BET SHE'S A GIRL. YOU NEVER SAID IT WAS A BOY!

IT LOOKS LIKE YOU DON'T EVEN CARE THAT I HAVEN'T WRITTEN YOU IN SO LONG.
I BET YOU COMPLETELY FORGOT ABOUT ME TO MAKE ROOM FOR YOUR NEW BEST FRIEND!

STILL.
THINKING OF YOU...

!
THIS IS IT.
THINKING OF YOU ALL ALONE...
TRYING TO GET THROUGH SCHOOL...
THIS IS THAT FEELING I HAD.
THE WAY SHE THOUGHT OF ME...
WELL, SHOOT.
...WHILE EVERYONE ELSE AVOIDED ME.

I GET REALLY PROUD OF YOU HANGING IN THERE.
SHE WAS THE ONLY ONE.
AND SHE SMILED AT ME!
OH.
ANYWAY.
I JUST WANTED TO TELL YOU THAT.
EVEN IF IT'S LAME.
AND ANOTHER THING.
STRETCH

.....
I WANT YOU TO WRITE ME BACK.
BYE FOR NOW!
BZZT

IF I HAD TO THINK OF A SINGLE ASPECT OF HER...
IT WAS HER SMILE.
Pfft!
HER SMILE WAS THE WEAPON THAT CUT THROUGH MY BARRIER.
She's as chipper as she ever was.
THAT'S MY ANSWER.
THAT'S WHY I LOVE HER.
!
I KNOW THAT VOICE.
HEY!
UGH.
I'M SO CRANKY TODAY.
DIIIING DOOOONG

THANKS FOR THE SHOW YESTERDAY, MAN.
...WHY AM I EVEN HIDING?
Now I'm even more annoyed.
ROLL ROLL
!
SENDA!
SIDE
WHAT A WITCH.
YOU DIDN'T HAVE TO GO SO EASY ON HER, THOUGH.
HA
HA!
IT WAS NICE TO SEE HER GET KNOCKED DOWN A PEG.
SHOW?
.....
YEAH, WITH SONOKO!
DON'T TALK ABOUT YOUR EX-GIRLFRIEND LIKE THAT.

SHE DE-SERVES YOUR RESPECT.
SHE CAN GET OVER HER INSECURITIES AND DO THE RIGHT THING.
YOU DIDN'T DESERVE HER.
I KNOW WHAT IT'S LIKE.
YOUR BEHAVIOR NOW SHOWS HOW ROTTEN A PERSON YOU ARE.
IF I DIDN'T HAVE AIUCHI'S SMILE TO GIVE ME STRENGTH...

I COULDN'T BE LIKE THIS.
I COULDN'T SMILE ON MY OWN.
LISTEN TO HER.
A STRONG GIRL PUSHING HER WAY INTO YOUR LIFE...
...CAN BE THE BEST THING TO EVER HAPPEN TO YOU!
SATA...!

I WATCHED YOUR DVD.
PAPA!
SATA SENT ME A DVD!
THE PARA-NOID KID?

ACTUALLY, I THOUGHT YOU'D FORGOTTEN ABOUT *ME*.
I'M SURPRISED YOU THOUGHT I'D FORGOTTEN ABOUT YOU.
YOU LEFT TOO DEEP AN IMPRESSION ON MY LIFE FOR THAT.
AIUCHI ...
ER...
RIGHT.

I HAVE SOMETHING TO TELL YOU.
AND I'M GOING TO TELL YOU PROPERLY.
AIUCHI, I...
YUI!
WE TALKED ABOUT THIS!
!
Don't rattle my cage!
I HOPE SHE GOT MY LETTER.

IT'S SONOKO.
Meow!
ぐいっ
AGH!
YUMENO!

LET ME IN YOUR LITTLE BOX--THERE'S ROOM FOR TWO IN THERE. ♡
Meee-eow!
DON'T EMULATE YUI AND HIS ANIMALISTIC PESTERING!
THERE THEY GO AGAIN.
JUST IGNORE THEM.
It's gotten boring.
Meow!

I HEARD YOUR SPEECH ABOUT STRONG GIRLS BEING A GOOD THING.
SO LET ME SMASH MY WAY INTO YOUR STERILE LITTLE WORLD. ♡

WOULD YOU *PLEASE* STOP THAT?!
NO
Heh heh.

BUT I HOPE, AND BELIEVE, THAT WE'RE BOTH FEELING THE SAME THING.

CLEAN FREAK, FULLY EQUIPPED EPISODE 3/END

EPISODE
4
KEEP OUT
KEEP OUT
KEEP OUT

My cat.

Return to the first panel.

YOU! IN THE SHIRT!
DON'T MIGRATE FROM YOUR LINE!
IF ALL OF YOU CAN'T STAY IN PROPER SINGLE FILE...
...THE AREAS I'VE STERILIZED WILL GET CONTAMINATED AGAIN!
STAY IN LINE!
Waiting in line to change shoes.
I REFUSE TO COMPROMISE THE EXIT'S STERILITY!
SATA SENDA, 1ST YEAR MIDDLE SCHOOL STUDENT. AUTUMN.
PARANOID ABOUT GERMS. WORKING AS THE SCHOOL'S BEAUTIFICATION COMMISSIONER (AND ENJOYING IT).
100% ETHANOL WILL MAKE SURE OF THAT!

LEAP
I WISH HE WOULD STOP YELLING.
KEEP AT IT, SOLDIERS!
RESPECT THE SPIRIT OF IN-DOOR SHOES, ONE OF THE CLEANEST TRA-DITIONS OF JAPANESE CULTURE!
ROOOOOOOOOAAAAAAAAAR
SQUEAK
SQUEAK
SQUEAK
Out of the way! Move!
Heavy!
SQUEAK
SQUEAK
SQUEAK
SQUEAK
SQUEAK
SQUEAK
SQUEAK
SQUEAK

I keep telling you I'm in N.Y., dummy! ♡
Dear Aiuchi, currently living in an unknown location.
I hope you're doing well. My obsessive-compulsive cleaning behavior that you curbed while you were here...
PHEW.
...has become my secret weapon in my new role as the school beautification commissioner.
*HIS DISORDER IS NOT EXACTLY SECRET.
A look of satisfaction behind the mask!
Zzzzzz.
THERE'S SO MUCH TO DO!
BRUSH
BRUSH

IF YOU HAVE TO SLEEP, DO IT ELSEWHERE! YOU'RE DIRECTLY IN THE WAY OF MY BEAUTIFICATION/ STERILIZATION!
I DON'T WANNA GO.
nyum nyum
GIMME FIVE MORE MINUTES...
MGGGNN...
I SHOULD'VE KNOWN I'D FIND YOU HERE, YUI.
WA HA HA HA HA!
ROLL ROLL ROLL
HOP
I LIKE HANGING OUT WITH YOU. ♡
His name is Yui Anzai.
Over the course of this year, this strange creature became my best friend.

※EVERYONE IS WEARING OUTSIDE SHOES.

BARON ...
SO...
GOOEY!
SORRY.
MUMBLE
MUMBLE
THE RABBIT'S FROM THE SCHOOL PEN.
MUMBLE
MUMBLE
IF EVERYTHING COULD BE SOLVED BY SAYING "SORRY," WE WOULDN'T NEED ETHANOL!
ARRRRGH!
GOOEY SAYS HE'LL RE-DO THE CLEANING.
IS THAT YOUR RABBIT, SOTSUGU KIRIYU?! ...AND DOES "GOOEY" REFER TO SOTSUGU?
Right?
CLEAN THIS FLOOR UNTIL YOU WOULD BE HAPPY TO LICK IT ON MY COMMAND!
THEN CLEAN! POLISH THIS AREA UNTIL YOU CAN SEE BRAZIL!
HE DID, DID HE?!
Before you see Brazil, you'll probably see the earth's core.

GET YOUR WHITES THEIR WHITEST!
The story of the Baron.
Woo-hoo!
I tried to use a lot of white in this chapter. Also, I wanted to make this fake laundry commercial.
GOOEY WANTS TO KNOW IF YOU'LL ACTUALLY LISTEN TO A COMPLAINT.
EXCUSE ME!
IF YOU HAVE A COMPLAINT, VOICE IT YOURSELF!
Wait, how much?
MUMBL
MUMBL
THAT'S PROBABLY IMPOSSIBLE.
MUMBLE
MUMBLE
IS BRAZIL EVEN OPPOSITE HERE?
MUMBLE
THEN HE SAID HE'LL TRY!
OF COURSE I WON'T.
STOP USING YUI AS YOUR VOICE PROXY.
YOU HAVE VOCAL CHORDS FOR A REASON! AND THE BIT ABOUT BRAZIL WAS JUST HYPERBOLE.
ARE YOU JEALOUS?
OF WHAT?!
That doesn't make sense!

BRUSH
BRUSH
GOOEY'S REALLY TIMID. DON'T BE SO HARD ON HIM.
HE CAN'T TALK IN A NORMAL VOICE.
YOU ARE JEALOUS!
NO!
BUT... REGARDLESS! YOU AREN'T HIS PERSONAL MICROPHONE!
NEVER MIND!
1-5
ALL RIGHT...
IT'S TIME FOR TODAY'S HOMEROOM TOPIC.
WE WOULD LIKE TO DISCUSS SENDA'S BEAUTIFICATION ACTIVITIES.
WHAT?!
SHAKE SHAKE
senda's beau...
Don't write it down!

Yeah!
SENDA'S DRUNK ON POWER. HIS RIDICULOUS RULES ARE MAKING US LATE FOR CLASS.
TOTALLY!
?!!
panic panic
DRUNK ON POWER?
ME! ME!
びょん
びょん
BEG YOUR PARDON?!
NO OBJECTIONS. AS THE ONLY CURRENT MEMBER OF THE ANIMAL CARE COMMITTEE, KIRIYU COULD USE THE HELP.
I CAN SWITCH WITH SATA! AND GOOEY THINKS SATA SHOULD BE PART OF THE ANIMAL CARE COMMITTEE.
And that isn't even your seat, Yui!
I OBJECT!
ENDA
Dear Aiuchi, wherever you are.

Due to a classroom conspiracy against me...
...I've been downgraded to the animal care committee.
I!
DON'T!
WANT TO!
GOOEY SAID HE WANTS YOU TO MEET SOMEBODY.
After school.
AND STOP PULLING ME!
You have the strength of a monster!
Nya Ha Ha!
MY JOB DOESN'T START UNTIL TOMORROW! AT LEAST LEAVE ME ALONE ON MY LAST DAY OF FREEDOM!
THE POOR GIRL.
I'M SUFFERING MYSELF! WHAT HELP COULD I...
...POSSIBLY--
SHE'S BEEN FEELING DOWN LATELY. MAYBE YOU CAN CHEER HER UP!

!
boin
YOU WERE JUST HAPPY THAT YOUR HUSBAND CAME BACK. RIGHT, BAR-ON?
THAT'S RIGHT, BARON! YOU SHOULDN'T JUMP ON EVERY-ONE!
THIS IS BARON, THE BUNNY I WANTED YOU TO MEET.

Ow...
プス
プス
UM...
BARON'S HUSBAND WAS JUST ADOPTED. I GUESS HE LOOKED LIKE YOU, SATA.
LET ME GET THIS STRAIGHT! YOU HAVE A FEMALE RABBIT NAMED "BARON."
robably oks like this.
AND I LOOK LIKE HER RABBIT USBAND. ARE YOU TRYING O HUMILIATE Y PARENTS?!
Or make them laugh at me?!
You!
Idiots!
WIPE WIPE
AW, C'MON.
YOU CAN'T BE MAD AT THIS WIDDLE FACE, SATA.
AND SHE OOOOOOOVES YOU.
ずいっ

SENDA...
PLEASE.
MUMBLE
MUMBLE
flap
flap
flap
PLEASE VISIT BARON EVERY DAY.
PUNCH PUNCH
MUMBLE
AFTER SEEING YOU, SENDA...
Sata's love hurts.
...BARON'S BEEN FEELING BETTER.
MUMBLE
IT'S BAD ENOUGH THAT THE CLASS GAVE ME DUTIES HERE.
SOB
BUT COME EVERY DAY?! NO, THANK YOU!
UGH!
YOU CAN'T FORCE ME TO LIKE SOMETHING THAT I HATE!

DON'T LOOK AT ME WITH THOSE EYES!
ON THE DAY OF MANDATORY ANIMAL CARE.
OVER THERE!
BUH-GAWK! FLAP FLAP
ARGH!
HOLD THOSE ANIMALS DOWN! EVERY SINGLE ONE OF THEM!
IF EVEN ONE OF THOSE BEASTS GETS NEAR ME...!
CRASH
LUCK
CLUCK
DON'T DRIVE ME TO DO SOMETHING WE'LL ALL REGRET!
RASH

KUUUH...
SHUU...
I THINK YOUR GERM SUIT IS OFFICIALLY TOO WEIRD NOW.
I CAN'T DO THIS ANYMORE!
SHOVEL
KA-CAW!
WEDNES-DAY.
NOOOO!
KA-CAW!
No!
Ew!
MON-DAY.
SPRITZ
Filth!
SPRITZ
SPRITZ
MICROBES!
SHUDDER
SHUDDER
1-5
TIME TO GO TO THE BARN AGAIN! LET'S BE EXTRA NICE TO THE CHICKENS THIS TIME.

BUT YOU HAVE TO GO! IT'S AN OFFICIAL COMMITTEE DAY.
MUMBLE
Stop it!
NO MORE!
YOU'RE TOO BUSY CUDDLING WITH THOSE DISGUSTING RABBITS!
YOU TWO DON'T EVEN HELP ME CLEAN THAT FILTHY BARN!
Selective memory.
Senda
BRUSH
BRUSH
RAR!
ガララ…
のそのそ
SLAM
NO!
WE'LL HELP YOU CLEAN. PROMISE!
MUMBLE
MUMBLE
I'M NOT GOING!
HUH?

TWITCH
GOOEY'S NOT AN AGGRESSIVE GUY.
BUT HE'S REALLY PUSHING THIS.
ガチャ
SATA...
YOU KNOW SOMETHING?
FREEZE
flap
flap
flap
!
IT'S OBVIOUSLY REALLY IMPORTANT TO HIM THAT YOU MAKE BARON HAPPY.

sproing
!
I DON'T CARE!
BESIDES, HE'S WAY TOO OVERPROTECTIVE OF THAT THING! IT'S JUST A RABBIT. IT'S NOT LIKE IT CAN DIE OF HEARTBREAK.
SLIDE
Senda
?!
BARON!

murmur
HUH?
WAS THAT KIRIYU?
HE SOUNDS LIKE A VOICE ACTOR.
I'VE NEVER HEARD HIS VOICE BEFORE.
MUMBLE
SHE'S NOT HERE?
That is a TV voice.
UM, NO.
SHE'S NOT HERE.
I-V
NOW WHAT...?!
BARON...!
...AND I THOUGHT SHE WENT TO YOU.
WHY?
SHE RAN AWAY...

……
AND SHE'S DUE TO GIVE BIRTH ANY DAY!
SATA!
ESPE-CIALLY IF SHE'S PREGNANT! HELP US LOOK?!
……
WE CAN'T LET ANY-THING HAPPEN TO HER!
!

SATA!
……
ガタッ
?
SATA!
ガラガラ
WHY ARE YOU GOING TO THE ROOF?!
BARON WON'T BE UP THERE!
ギイ…
WE'LL BE ABLE TO LOOK OVER MORE GROUND FROM HIGH UP.

THERE SHE IS!
LOOK OUT...!
WHY?!
!
boing

Ah!

DON'T!
PANIC
PANIC
PANIC
HER BABIES ARE GONNA FALL OUT IF YOU HOLD HER LIKE THAT!
!!
The rabbit's been caught with bare hands!
PANIC
PANIC
PANIC
YOU'LL MAKE THE BABIES POP OUT OF HER MOUTH!
NO!
WHAT?!
!!
Yui stopped making sense.

DASH
Gooey! Sata was hugging Baron!
Y-Y-YUI!
DASH
FLAP
FLAP
THAT WAS VERY RECKLESS, YOUNG LADY.
I-V
I GET IT.
I GET IT! STOP...DO-ING THAT! YOU'RE SENDING GERMS AIRBORNE!

I'LL VISIT YOU IN THE BARN.
EVERY DAY.
しゅっぴん
YO!

MEOW!
GOOD AFTERNOON, FRIEND!
.....
UM ...
MUMBLE
TH-THANKS FOR SAVING BARON... YESTER-DAY.
MUMBLE
WHAT ARE YOU TWO DOING?
PLAYING PRISONER.
WHAP
HEY!
DID HE CAPTURE YOU OR SOMETH--
KYA HA HA HA HA HA!
KYA HA HA HA HA HA!
STOP ACTING LIKE SOME SORT OF MUPPET MONSTER.
UM ...
THANK YOU FOR YESTERDAY!
SENDA!

...SO YOU DO HAVE YOUR OWN VOICE.
YOU SHOULD USE IT.
I CAN'T USUALLY HEAR YOU WHEN YOU'RE MUMBLING TO YOURSELF.
.....
I MUCH PREFER THE LOUDER YOU.
I-V

How are you, Aiuchi?

The punchline

I took a photo for you.
Sotsugyo Kiriyu (has a voice fit for a movie star)
Me.
Baron (mother of seven)
Yui Anzai (monster)
!
SO THESE ARE SENDA'S FRIENDS...!
.....
TAKE A LOOK AT THE BACK, SWEET-HEART.
Ha ha ha.

CLEAN FREAK, FULLY EQUIPPED EPISODE 4/END

Thanks for reading this volume through to the end. This is Tobi-something something. I appreciate your support!
I thought I'd just fill the bonus sections with pictures, but then I realized putting text in might give the contents more weight, so I'll write a little something.
No need to let me bore you, though. You can skip the writing if you want.

About Episode 1
This was the story that received the Athena award. I'm so thankful...
Kyoto's raw fumochi is really delicious.

↑Completely unrelated.
Aiuchi was very difficult for me to draw, so I cried every time she showed up.

About Episode 2
This was the story that led to my debut. I'm so thankful...
I never dreamt that I would get to draw a sequel to a weird story about an OCD clean boy. I never dreamt I could get one chapter published.
With lots of dark tones, this episode is really busy, and it's hard to see what's going on. I was told I have a lot of terrible drawing habits.

About Episode 3
It's the Sonoko story. I'm so thankful.
Black tone was absolutely not used (extreme).
And this episode was drawn while I was watching TV--so when I looked back on my work, it was just unbelievable. "What's wrong with this fork?!" ←It wasn't just that...
(The pictures also lost their momentum.)
And the chins! The chins were just horrible!

About Episode 4
Baron's story. (I insist on calling it that.)
I was so traumatized by my earlier chins, I compensated by using a lot of white in this chapter? Not exactly. In this particular episode, I challenged myself to use as much white as possible. (Such unnecessary challenges.)
During the initial plot, it was very dark, but once I took away the darkness, the episode resulted in what you see published here.
While I was drawing episodes 2-4, I had to say good-bye to my grandfather and bunny, but other than that, it was a fulfilling year for me.
The next 16 pages are a story that received the HMC award...I'm so thankful.
While drawing it, there were a lot of things that were missing (especially my mind).
But I was serious about it at the time!

That is all.

There were a lot of open spaces throughout these author's notes, but I'm not sure I've filled them with good things and/or substance.

KASUMI JUNIOR HIGH
CHAN-CELLOR!
Home Ec Room
AFTER THE LATEST FIRE, MORE PARENTS THAN EVER ARE BEGGING TO WITHDRAW THEIR CHILDREN!
KEEP OUT KEEP
THE INJURY CHANGED EVERY-THING.
THESE AREN'T THE SMALL FIRES OF THE PAST. WE CAN'T HANDLE THEM THE WAY WE USED TO!
Hm.
SLUP
YOU'RE RIGHT, MR. OSOKAWA.
..BUT I HEARD THERE ARE "SPECIAL" INDIVIDUALS FOR HANDLING ISSUES LIKE THIS.
I'M NOT SURE OF THE DETAILS ...
I KNEW THE TRUTH.
I KNEW BECAUSE IT ALWAYS HAPPENED NEAR ME.
IT WAS CONNECT-ED TO MY ANGER.
RUMBLE

SHALL WE CALL ONE UP?
HE GOES BY THE CODE NAME "DISPATCH STUDENT."
派遣学生
■ Dispatch Student ■

....WAS A BAD DAY.
I...
I'M NOT INTERESTED IN GIRLS.
DEFINITELY.
WILL YOU GO OUT WITH ME?
WAIT.
YOU DON'T KNOW?
UM... JYUN?
TODAY.
I'VE LIKED YOU FOR A LONG TIME.
TODAY...
I'm not wearing boys' clothes because I want to!
I CAN'T BEAR IT!
BEAR IT, JYUN! YOU CAN... BEAR...IT...
ARRRRGH!
RUMBLE.
UGH! WHATEVER!!
MY BROOM STARTED TO...BURN ALL OF A SUDDEN.
OW.
!
Burn?
GYAH!
WHY ARE YOU DRESSED LIKE THAT? DO YOU LIKE CONFUSING EVERYONE?!

WHO IS THAT?
WHY ARE YOU WEARING A *MALE* SCHOOL UNIFORM?
SO...
SORRY!
WHY ARE YOU APOLO-GIZING?
UM...
!!
YOU...YOU CAN TELL THAT I'M A GIRL?
YEAH, IT'S PRETTY OBVIOUS.
HEY!
SQUEEZE

WELL.
WE'LL MEET AGAIN.
ひらり
HUH?!
I-I CAN'T BELIEVE THIS!
MUMBLE
MORN-ING, JYUN.
MORN-ING.
I'VE NEVER SEEN HIS FACE BEFORE, AND HE TURNS OUT TO BE A TRANSFER STUDENT!
THAT PER-VERT!
WHEN I SEE HIM AGAIN, I'M GONNA TURN HIM UPSIDE-DOWN AND YANK OUT HIS HAIR.
WAIT!
HE TRANSFERRED INTO *THIS* CLASS?!
EEEK!
OU KNOW KANZAKI ALREADY, JYUN? I'M JEALOUS.

NO!
This isn't happening!
I JUST BUMPED INTO HIM! UNFORTUNATELY!
BUT WE'RE ALREADY VERY CLOSE. PHYSICALLY.
AAAH!
THERE'S A FIRE!
AND IT'S COMING FROM AMADA'S DESK!
BA-DUMP
IT'S SO... HOT...!
PUNCH
Shut
PUNCH
Your mouth, Kanzaki!
Whoa, whoa.
...Scandal. Love it!
RUMBLE.
IT HURTS.
I CAN'T... TAKE IT!
GET A FIRE EXTINGUISHER!
BLOP
BLOP
NO! NO!
IT'S NOT ME!
DASH
Kyaaa!
GET OUTSIDE!
Move the other desks away!

PLEASE STOP!
NO!
AND IT'S NOT JUST BECAUSE I'M TALL, OR BECAUSE I HAVE CHISELED FEATURES FROM BEING MIXED RACE.
I'VE ALWAYS LOOKED LIKE A MAN.
NO!
MR. HOSOI!
!
Hey, it's Futoi!
YOUR SKIRT IS TOO LONG.
!!
HMMM? AREN'T YOU BREAKING SCHOOL RULES WITH THIS?
LET HER GO!
I NEED TO EXAMINE YOU MORE CLOSELY.
IF SKIRT LENGTH IS AN ISSUE...
...PICK ON SOMEONE YOUR OWN SIZE WHO'S HAPPY TO SPIT ON THAT RULE.
KIRIYU.
I GUESS PEOPLE SEE THAT AS MACHO OR SOMETHING.
I'M ALSO PRETTY AGGRESSIVE.

SNIP
SNIP
Home Ec Room
fab
fab
KIRIYU...
I SEE.
COME TO THE GUIDANCE ROOM AFTER SCHOOL.
MALE STUDENTS AREN'T SUPPOSED TO HAVE LONG HAIR.
AND THIS!
YOU'RE WEARING A FEMALE UNIFORM.
TAKE IT OFF IMMEDIATELY.
ON TOP OF THAT...
...I'VE GOT A HOT TEMPER.
RUMBLE
I-IF YOU DON'T WANT THIS TO GET YOU IN TROUBLE...
...YOU HAVE TO DO WHAT I SAY!
CRACKLE
CRACKLE
huff
huff
...?
RUMBLE

HUFF
HUFF
ガタン
NO...
RUMBLE
IT WASN'T ME. IT WAS JUST COINCI-DENCE!
RUMBLE
ゴオオオオオ
COINCIDENCE?
THAT WAS THE HOME EC ROOM...
THEY ALREADY USE FIRE THERE!
YES, IT WAS!
"WAS IT COINCI-DENCE THAT THE BOY WHO WAS INSULTING YOU GOT BURNED?"
RUM-BLE
I-I'm sorry! Mommyyyyy!
Did you call me "butch" as an insult? What's wrong with being butch?
AIEEEEEEEE!
JERK

THEN WHY DID YOU APOLOGIZE WHEN I SAID MY BROOM HAD STARTED TO BURN?
FINE.
COINCIDENCE!
"WHAT ABOUT THE LOCKER THAT STARTED SIZZLING WHEN YOU FOUGHT SOME BULLY?"
YES!
I DIDN'T DO ANY-THING!
"ALL OF IT?"
"THEN THERE WAS THIS..."
"...AND THIS."
YOU START FIRES, JYUN.
YOU JUST DON'T WANT TO ADMIT IT.
I...I DON'T --
WHA...
KANZAKI-?!
?
THIS IS THE WOMEN'S BATHROOM!
YOU ALREADY KNOW THE TRUTH.
Closed for cleanin

THAT'S NOT FUNNY --
YOU'RE A WITCH?
I CAN PROVE IT, IF YOU WANT.
TH-THAT'S IMPOS-SIBLE!
NOTHING'S IMPOSSI-BLE. TAKE IT FROM A WITCH.
...IS BECAUSE YOUR HAND POSITION IS ALL WRONG.
I CAN TEACH YOU A SPELL.
THE REASON YOU'RE SETTING RANDOM FIRES...
?
Come here.
...CALL OUT MY NAME.
NEXT TIME YOU'RE ABOUT TO DO SOMETHING DRASTIC...
...?

KIRIYU?
THAT'S THE WOMEN'S RESTROOM.
……!
NO.
BUT IF I REALLY STARTED A FIRE HERE…
"YOU START FIRES, JYUN."
…MAYBE I SHOULD SHOW YOU HOW?
IF YOU DON'T KNOW HOW TO US THE MEN'S RESTROOM …
"…CALL OUT MY NAME."
HE…
!

"KIRI-YU?"
CLICK
THAT'S THE WOM-EN'S REST-OOM."
HELP ME!
KANZAKI!
I'M PORT-S YOU WO!
YOU! BOY! YOU WERE IN THE WOMEN'S RESTROOM TOO!
I GET IT--YOU AND KIRIYU WERE DOING SOMETHING ILLICIT IN THERE!
!
You what?!
WHA...
I RECORD-ED THE WHOLE THING.
SLAM
"IF YOU DON'T KNOW HOW TO USE THE MEN'S REST-ROOM..."
CLICK
I WOULD ENJOY BEING ILLICIT WITH JYUN.
What a waste.
Seriously...
WELL.
WHICH CLASS ARE--
HEE.
BUT NOT NOW.
I'M ON A MISSION.
?!
HOW 'BOUT A ROUND OF APPLAUSE FOR YOUR HERO.

A P-PIPSQUEAK LIKE YOU?!
ALL IT TAKES IS A CALL.
YUP.
FROM THE STUDENTS WHO ARE PREPPED TO HANDLE ANY PROBLEMS ON ANY CAMPUS.
...THE SPECIALIST WE SENT FOR?!
WAIT. ARE YOU ...
MAYBE THAT WAS A SECRET.
OOP.
...THE DISPATCH STUDENTS!
MISSION ACCOMPLISHED.
GIVE US A KISS.
Kthanxbye.
I WAS SENT TO STOP FIRES ...
THE NATION'S SUPER SECRET SCHOOL...
MUMBLE
...AND INVESTIGATE YOU, MR. HOSOI.
HEY.
THAT...THING EARLIER. YOU WERE KIDDING ABOUT CASTING SPELLS.
YOU THINK I WAS KIDDING?
HEY, JYUN. SHORT TIME NO SEE.

THAT SPELL WORKS WITH ANY NAME.
YOU'RE ACTUALLY PRETTY EASY TO TALK TO.
YEAH. BUT THANKS.
TOO BAD YOU LIKE ME.
I HAVE TO TRANSFER AGAIN SOON.
!
BUT LET ME LEAVE YOU WITH A LITTLE SOME-THING.
!
SO HE'S SAYING I CAN'T FIX VERY PROB-LEM ON MY OWN.
"HELP ME!"
WHAT?
YOU'RE NUTS.
OR NEI-THER.
A WITCH?
A HERO?
WHO ARE YOU, ANYWAY?
HM.

DISPATCH STUDENT/END

FOR THOSE PEOPLE...

...WHO THINK THAT "CLEAN FREAK" IS NOW OVER. (EVEN THOUGH IT'S NOT.)

If Sata were a clean freak and paranoid about the universe.

It doesn't really matter, but "gya ha ha" makes him sound evil.

his happened in the middle of class, more children would be hurt.

It happened to be friday the 13th today.

WHY DOES YUMENO HAVE A CRUSH ON ME, ANYWAY?
AND SHE KNOWS SO MUCH ABOUT ME EVEN THOUGH WE HAVEN'T TALKED IN YEARS.
Twee
Twee Too
WE'RE MOVING TO THE MUSIC ROOM NEXT. LET'S WALK TOGETHER, SENDA!
EEK!
WHAT OW?!
SPriZ
Imaginary Stalker.
♥ Ho ho ho!♥
I WOULDN'T GO THROUGH YOUR GARBAGE IF YOU PAID ME!
G-GOING THROUGH SOMEONE'S TRASH IS UNSANITARY!
Don't do it!
I oughta throw you in the trash!
But she probably does follow him home.
I'm a classy lady!

SENDA!
OOF!
YOUR SMILE IS SO BRIGHT!
YOU'RE LIKE THE SUN! SO MUCH, IN FACT, THAT YOUR CHARM WILL EVENTUALLY CAUSE ME TO COMBUST!
SINGE
Senda
BUT I DON'T THE MIND. ONLY PROB-LEM...
Light!
Give us Light!
Around here.
Light!
AND OP-PORTUNISTS WILL WANT TO CONTROL HER LIGHT TO PROFIT FROM LIGHT-DEPRIVED CLIMATES!
...IS THAT THE REST OF THE WORLD WILL GANG UP ON HER BECAUSE OF HER MAGIC POWER!
Aiyee!
I WOULD NEVER SEE HER AGAIN, LET ALONE HAVE THE OPPOR-TUNITY TO BE VAPORIZED BY THE HEAT HER BEAUTIFUL SMILE RADIATES!

·X· Children, absolutely don't try this at home. ♥

This is trouble! For lots of reasons!

OCD cleanliness and general paranoia seem to be disorders that go hand in hand...but the previous comics are all side-stories unrelated to the plot. Oh, and even though I doubt anyone cares, I'll list some character heights here because I have some space.

Senda →6th grade: 153cm (5'0")
7th grade: 168cm (5'6") ←
At his growth spurt (seriously?)

Aiuchi →143cm (4'8")
She probably hasn't changed.
At least, she doesn't look it.

Yui →148cm (4'10")

Sonoko →145cm (4'9")

Sotsugu →175cm (5'9") And still growing!

I do have the characters' family structures all set up, but nobody cares, right? As a side note, Yui's living with his dad. He hasn't made an appearance, though.

Whatever! And another note:

← Yazaki in 7th grade. He seems to have transformed into something... He's in class 1.

By the way, part 2.

I wanted Sata's older sister, Sara, to make an appearance in this book, but she couldn't due to the limited number of pages. She's one year older than him, 170 cm tall (5'7").

This isn't seaweed!

I just felt like drawing totally random stuff.

How to make your own Senda Unit.

Things to prepare:

Portable closet
Clear plastic
Wheels (4)
Mop
Plastic tape
A complete lack of shame

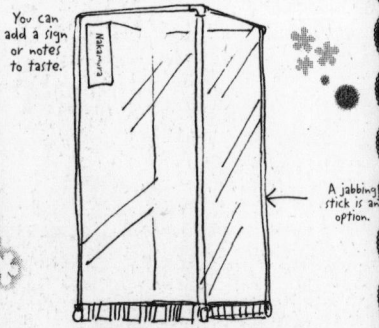

And it's made like that! Easy as pie! (Ignore the fact that I didn't actually include any instructions here.) Now you can take it to school!

*Note: The added benefit of this unit is you will get top priority for emergency meetings from all guidance counselors in your area.

Please ignore that I just shouted that out loud. I like fantasy stuff, but it's not like I'm obsessed with it...as you can see on the right, I just want to draw all kinds of stories. But there a lot of ways to fulfill that dream, so I need to push forward and work.
But there are also particular things that I love!
Like sexy macho men...
Bunnies that look like pudding...
Wolves.
I just like any kind of character who can show a little skin. That's why I like summer. So, with my hero in this series being a clean freak and all, I was conflicted on how to better expose his skin for the camera. (Just let him cover up!) Heck, it was difficult just to get him to show his face, and as a result, the Senda Unit was created.

But I hate drawing straight edges, so I was always cursing when I tried. Speaking of weaknesses, next to drawing backgrounds, I don't like screen tone. I use it in random, irrational ways, and the picture turns out just as irrational. I'm also not keen on drawing small objects and faces. Not that I have a good specialty... just weakness. One of these days...

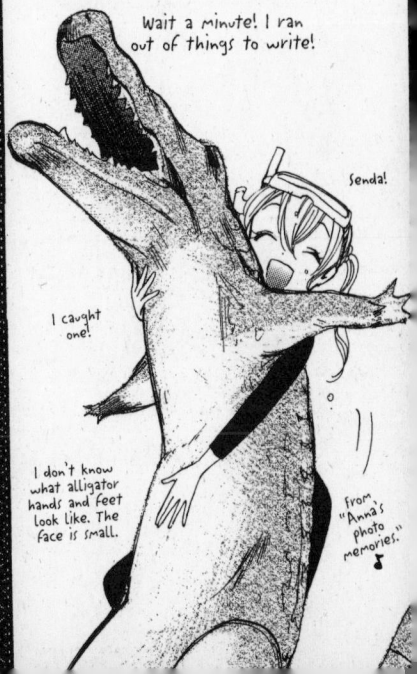

I actually wanted to put a bonus comic strip here, but I realized that there wasn't a single panel in this book that was typical of a shoujo manga. I tried to fix that here, but this section also ended up covered in my scribbles. Thank you very much for reading the first volume of Clean Freak all the way to the end. Thanks to everyone's support, I was able to draw/write complete nonsense in the author's notes too. I'm hoping that I will be able to live my life to successfully express my gratitude to everyone.

To everyone in the Nakamura Family. Thank you. Thank you.

To my friends. Thanks for all your attention! Please keep reading!

To N-sama. You're really wonderful! I'm sorry to rely on you so much... the cover made me laugh! Thank you!

To T-sama. Thank you very much for sticking with me even when my story ideas suck. I love you!

To everyone who was involved. I'm indebted to you all! Thank you very much! I know I'll need further assistance in the future!

And especially, everyone else! All the letters I received have been stored with great care! I apologize for not being able to send out replies as quickly as before. Thank you! Thank you!

PARANOIA BOY, FULLY FAILING/END

THANKS TO HIS TRAUMATIC CHILDHOOD INCIDENT, SATA SENDA IS COMPULSIVELY CLEAN, BUT CAN HE REALLY CONTINUE GOING THROUGH LIFE IN HIS OWN PERSONAL BUBBLE (LITERALLY)? THE FUN CONTINUES AS THE NEW YEAR APPROACHES, SENDA HAS SOME NEW EXPERIENCES (AND A RUN-IN WITH HIS OLD TEACHER), AND ENJOYS THE COMPANY OF HIS NEW FRIENDS...BUT HOW WILL THINGS CHANGE WHEN AIUCHI MAKES HER STUNNING RETURN TO JAPAN?!

?
ム
ス

DOWNLOAD THE REVOLUTION.

Get the free TOKYOPOP app for manga, anytime, anywhere!

12,000 MILES...20 CITIES...8 WEEKS...
6 STUDENTS...5 FAN CONS...ONE SEARCH...
AND A WHOOOOLE LOT OF POCKY...

WATCH IT WEEKLY AT
WWW.HULU.COM

PRODUCED BY TOKYOPOP

WWW.GREATESTOTAKU.COM

hulu

BE SURE TO VISIT WWW.TOKYOPOP.COM/SHOP FOR
EVERYTHING YOU COULD EVER WANT!

PUTTING THE VAN IN VANQUISH

WATCH IT FOR FREE ON HULU.COM!

STARRING NARUTO VOICE ACTOR YURI LOWENTHAL

VAN VON HUNTER

TOKYOPOP presents a SIDI LEVY STEVEN CALCOTE film YURI LOWENTHAL in "VAN VON HUNTER"
HEATHER MARIE MARSDEN TRAVIS STEVENS
MIKE SCHWARK & RON KAUFFERSEIN
SIDI LEVY & STEVEN CALCOTE
SHILO KAWAMURI
REM COHAN
TOKYOPOP

OFFICIAL SELECTION FANTASIA 2010

hulu

TOKYOPOP

FOR MORE INFORMATION VISIT: www.TOKYOPOP.com

STOP!

This is the back of the book. You wouldn't want to spoil a great en

This book is printed "manga-style," in the authentic Japanese right-to-le format. Since none of the artwork has been flipped or altered, readers get to experience the story just as the creator intended. You've been asking for it, so TOKYOPOP® delivered: authentic, hot-off-the-press, and far more fun!

DIRECTIONS

If this is your first time reading manga-style, here's a quick guide to help you understand how it works.

It's easy... just start in the top right panel and follow the numbers. Have fun, and look for more 100% authentic manga from TOKYOPOP®!